Excel 2019
The IF Functions

EASY EXCEL ESSENTIALS 2019 BOOK 4

M.L. HUMPHREY

CONTENTS

Introduction

The *Easy Excel Essentials 2019* series of titles are for intermediate-level users who want to focus on one specific topic such as PivotTables, Charts, Conditional Formatting, or the IF Functions.

The content of each title is extracted from either *Excel 2019 Intermediate* or *Excel 2019 Formulas & Functions* which cover intermediate-level Excel topics in more detail.

These books are written using Excel 2019 and assuming that a user is working in that program. If you are using an older version of Excel, the *Easy Excel Essentials* series may be a better choice since it was written using Excel 2013 and for a more general audience of Excel users.

With that introduction, let's dive into what I like to refer to as the IF Functions.

IF Functions

The IF Functions are a powerful set of functions that allow you to make calculations (SUM, AVERAGE, COUNT, MIN, or MAX) on a range of values only when a set of criteria have been met.

So they only SUM when the customer is from Alaska and bought Widgets. Or they only take the MIN value when the transaction occurred after January 1, 2020.

Essentially they combine IF or IFS, which we'll cover first, and the underlying function into one nice little bundle.

In Excel 2019, Excel introduced MINIFS and MAXIFS to what it already had, which was SUMIFS, AVERAGEIFS, and COUNTIFS.

SUMIFS, AVERAGEIFS, and COUNTIFS were upgraded versions of SUMIF, AVERAGEIF, and COUNTIF

The reason I bring this up is because of backwards compatibility. I don't want you to do what I once did which is use SUMIF when it came out only to find out that my client didn't have the same version of Excel and so couldn't use the worksheet I'd designed for them.

Be sure before you use these highly valuable functions that you can use them in the setting you need to use them in.

If not, you can recreate what they do with the underlying function (SUM, COUNT, etc.), nested IF functions and possibly a cascading series of steps.

I'm not going to walk through that here, though, because this book is about Excel 2019. So I am going to assume that you are only working in Excel 2019 or with others who are also working in Excel 2019 or newer versions and so have full access to these functions.

I'm also not going to cover SUMIF, AVERAGEIF, or COUNTIF because their "plural" cousins can do everything they can.

Alright? Let's dive in with IFS, which is also new in Excel 2019 but incredibly useful for conditional calculations.

The IFS Function

Notation: IFS(logical_test1, value_if_true1,…)

Excel Definition: Checks whether one or more conditions are met and returns a value corresponding to the first TRUE condition.

This is another function that was new with Excel 2019 and as far as I can tell can completely replace the IF function. But if you need backwards compatibility then you'll need to work with the IF function instead (which will be discussed briefly later).

The IF function was always one of my favorite functions, if such a thing can exist, so I'm certain that I will also love IFS.

IFS at its most basic lets you write a formula that says, "If X happens return Y, otherwise return Z." That's pretty simple. Powerful but simple.

But the reason I always loved the IF function was because I could nest them. So I could say, "If X happens, return Y. If X doesn't happen, but G does, then return H. And if neither X nor G happens, then return Z."

And I could keep going and going and going with that until I had twenty possible outcomes. I won't deny that it was very tricky to build a nested IF function. That's where my warnings about matching up your opening and closing parens come from, because if you don't it all turns to mush with nested IF functions.

But the beauty of IFS is that it is designed to make it easier to build a nested IF function. No more keeping track of a million closing parens.

Let's walk through some examples.

First we'll build a simple function to give free shipping to any customer who spends at least $25. Any customer who spends less than $25 will pay 5% in shipping costs.

To calculate our shipping cost, we write that as

$$=IFS(A1>=25,0,TRUE,A1*0.05)$$

Let's break that down.

The first part, the IF part of our first condition, is A1>=25. We're saying that if the customer's purchase in Cell A1 is greater than (>) OR equal to (=) 25 then we want the first outcome.

We then place that first outcome after the comma. In this case that's 0.

Which makes the THEN part of our first outcome 0. If the customer's purchase is equal to or greater than 25, then don't charge for shipping.

That leaves us with the third part, our ELSE portion of the decision tree.

Because this is the IFS function and we could list out ten of these conditions before we get to the end we have to put TRUE to tell Excel this is the closing condition, otherwise Excel won't know we're at the end.

So the next entry is TRUE and then there's a comma and then we have our calculation of the shipping cost when the transaction is for less than $25.

And that's

$$A1*0.05$$

Notice that for the calculation A1*.05 we don't have to use quotation marks. (Unlike some other functions where you do.)

Also note here that we are calculating the *shipping charge*, not the customer's transaction cost. If we wanted the total customer cost we would use A1*1.05 for that last section and A1 for the earlier value.

Okay. That was a basic IFS function. One condition, two possible outcomes.

The complexity level ratchets up when you start to nest conditions. Let's look at the basic format of an IFS function again.

It's IF-THEN-ELSE, right? IF x, THEN y, ELSE z.

Or IF-THEN-OTHERWISE. IF x, THEN y, OTHERWISE z.

When you start to add conditions using the IFS function it becomes a situation where you're saying, "If this, then that, but if it's not this but instead this other thing, then…but if it's not that other thing either but it is this thing over here, then…" and so on and so on and so on.

You can write an IFS function with 127 different conditions in it. (Although Excel and I both would not recommend doing so because the order in which you add your conditions is crucial and that would be really hard to get right.)

Confused yet? It sounds horribly complicated doesn't it?

Let's walk through an example which should help this come clear.

We're going to build an IFS function that calculates a customer discount that escalates as customers spend more and more money.

If a customer spends at least $25 they get $5 off. If they spend $75 they get $10 off. If they spend $100 they get $15 off. And if they spend $250 they get $25 off.

For me the easiest way to do this is to build a table of the values and discounts and work from there. Here it is with our discount table up top and our test values down below.

	A	B	C
1	**Order Amount**	**Discount Amount**	
2	$25.00	$5.00	
3	$75.00	$10.00	
4	$100.00	$15.00	
5	$250.00	$25.00	
6			
7	**Customer Spend**	**Rebate**	**Formula in Column B**
8	$10.25		
9	$27.50		
10	$74.95		
11	$100.00		
12	$225.00		
13	$250.00		

We have the cut-off order amounts in Cells A2 through A5 and the discounts the customer will receive at each level in Cells B2 through B5.

Below that starting in Cell A8 are the values we're going to use to test our discount formula.

Let's start building our function. Our first condition is that if they spend under $25 they receive no discount.

We write that as

$$=IFS(A8<A2,0$$

The next condition is that if they spend less than $75 (the value in Cell A3) but at least $25 (which we've already determined is true with the first part of the function) they will get $5 off (the value in Cell B2).

Let's add that to our formula:

=IFS(A8<A2,0,A8<A3,B2

(Note that because of the way I built my table the order amount and the discount amount are pulling from different rows in this example.)

From this point onward we just keep adding each layer of discount until we've added all but the last one:

=IFS(A8<A2,0,A8<A3,B2,**A8<A4,B3,A8<A5,B4,**

At which point we add our final closing condition which is going to be TRUE,B5 and we close it out with a closing paren.

Adding in $ signs to fix our table reference so that we can copy this formula down to the rest of the cells we end up with:

=IFS(A8<$A$2,0,A8<$A$3,$B$2,A8<$A$4,$B$3,A8<$A$5,$B$4, TRUE,$B$5)

That looks like a complex mess, but it's actually simpler than the same formula using an IF function because with an IF function we would have had to insert an IF between every change in condition and made sure that all our closing parens were in the right place. Here we just have one function to do the same thing.

Here are our results and the formula for each row.

7	Customer Spend	Rebate	Formula in Column B
8	$10.25	$0.00	=IFS(A8<$A$2,0,A8<$A$3,$B$2,A8<$A$4,$B$3,A8<$A$5,$B$4,TRUE,$B$5)
9	$27.50	$5.00	=IFS(A9<$A$2,0,A9<$A$3,$B$2,A9<$A$4,$B$3,A9<$A$5,$B$4,TRUE,$B$5)
10	$74.95	$5.00	=IFS(A10<$A$2,0,A10<$A$3,$B$2,A10<$A$4,$B$3,A10<$A$5,$B$4,TRUE,$B$5)
11	$100.00	$15.00	=IFS(A11<$A$2,0,A11<$A$3,$B$2,A11<$A$4,$B$3,A11<$A$5,$B$4,TRUE,$B$5)
12	$225.00	$15.00	=IFS(A12<$A$2,0,A12<$A$3,$B$2,A12<$A$4,$B$3,A12<$A$5,$B$4,TRUE,$B$5)
13	$250.00	$25.00	=IFS(A13<$A$2,0,A13<$A$3,$B$2,A13<$A$4,$B$3,A13<$A$5,$B$4,TRUE,$B$5)

I only had to write the formula once because after I'd finished in Cell B8 and the $ signs were in place, I could just copy and paste down to the other cells.

Note that the A8 references in the above formula did not get $ signs because that's the cell reference that needs to change with each row. But all the others did because they needed to be fixed references.

Also, always remember with an IFS function to check the edge cases. In this instance that's values of $25, $75, $100, and $250, to make sure that they are falling into the correct category.

The way I just showed you is one way to write that function to get the result we needed, but I could have just as easily written it using greater than and equals to instead.

Let's do that now for just the first two conditions, a discount of $5 at $25 and a discount of $10 at $75. In this case we have to start with the highest discount first to get it to work.

So our first condition is if the customer spend (in Cell A8) is greater than or equal to our highest order level ($75 in Cell A3) then they will get our highest discount ($10 in Cell B3):

$$=IFS(A8>=A3,B3$$

If that's not true, then if the spend is greater than our next level spend cutoff (in this case $25 in Cell A2) then they will get our next level discount (in this case $5 in Cell B2):

$$=IFS(A8>=A3,B3,A8>=A2,B2,$$

And if that's not true either then we're out of discounts and we close it off with TRUE and a discount of zero.

$$=IFS(A8>=A3,B3,A8>=A2,B2,TRUE,0)$$

Note how in this version the customer spend and discount amount were pulled from the same row for each discount level.

Okay.

Don't get upset if you write one of these wrong the first time, I usually do. I did on this last one. Because it was easier for me to mentally build from the lowest level up like we did the first time rather than start on the highest level and work my way down like we had to on this one.

I just keep faith that this is all logic, pure and simple, and that if something isn't working the way it should it's because I haven't mapped out the steps properly and I just need to keep trying until I figure out where I went wrong.

If you really, really get stuck, pull out a piece of paper and starting drawing one of those branching decision trees. You know, "we started here, branch one is this, it got us here, branch two is this, it gets us there," etc. until you've drawn out the whole thing.

For example, with the function we just wrote: We started with any purchase amount. If that amount was greater than or equal to $75 that's our first branch and it took us to a discount of $10. But if it wasn't $75 or more then we take the other branch Okay. Now what? What happens down that branch? If it's equal to or more than $25 then we go down a branch that takes us to a discount of $5. But if that branch isn't true, where does that take us? To a discount of zero.

It's a little bit of mental gymnastics. Some take to it better than others. But if you can master it, I personally think the IFS function and its related functions (COUNTIFS, SUMIFS, etc.) are some of the most useful functions in Excel.

The IF Function

Notation: IF(logical_test, [value_if_true], [value_if_false])

Excel Definition: Checks whether a condition is met, and returns one value if TRUE, and another value if FALSE.

We're not going to spend a lot of time on the IF function in this book because the IFS function should be able to replace it and if you're new to Excel I encourage you to learn the IFS function instead.

But I'm so grounded in using the IF function and other people you work with may be as well, that it deserves a quick pass.

So the IF function at its most basic lets you set up an IF-THEN-ELSE or IF-THEN-OTHERWISE set of conditions just like the IFS function did.

A basic IF function requires less inputs than the basic IFS function. Let's take the shipping example we used for IFS

$$=IFS(A1>=25,0,TRUE,A1*0.05)$$

That was saying that if the value in A1 is greater than or equal to 25, our shipping cost should be zero, otherwise it should be 5% of the value in A1.

With IF that same formula is:

$$=IF(A1>=25,0, A1*0.05)$$

We don't need that extra TRUE in there to tell Excel this is the last condition. But where IFS shines compared to IF is in the more complex nested functions.

Let's take that final sample from IFS that we used:

$$=IFS(A8>=A3,B3,A8>=A2,B2,TRUE,0)$$

That was saying that if the value in Cell A8 is greater than or equal to the value in Cell A3 then return a value of B3. ELSE if the value in A8 is greater than or equal to A2 return a value of B2. OTHERWISE return a value of 0.

I wrote that with the ELSE and the OTHERWISE in the descriptions because every time it's an ELSE if you're working with a basic IF function you need to put in a new IF function in your formula. Like so:

$$=IF(A8>=A3,B3,IF(A8>=A2,B2,0))$$

See that I have two IF functions in there? And that I had to close it out with two closing parens, one to close the first IF function and one to close the second IF function?

Okay. So those are some simple examples of IF versus IFS. If you're new to Excel just learn IFS.

But if you do enough in Excel you may run into a very complex IF function written by someone like me who has used them for years. And if you need to troubleshoot that function I want to give you a few tips on how to approach that.

Here's an incredibly complex nested IF function:

$$=IF(A22>\$A\$2,IF(A22>\$A\$3,IF(A22>\$A\$4,$$
$$IF(A22>\$A\$5,IF(A22>\$A\$5,\$B\$5),\$B\$4),\$B\$3),\$B\$2),0)$$

(This is an example written in what I find the harder format for nested IF functions because each new IF function is added in the middle of the formula rather than the end which makes it much harder to see where each IF function actually starts and ends..)

What I do if I have to troubleshoot a mess like this is remove everything except the first IF function. So I take that mess up there and I make it:

$$=IF(A22>\$A\$2,"THEN X",0)$$

Everything in the middle is irrelevant until I make sure that the first part works. If it does, then I drop that part of the formula away and check the next part with everything that isn't part of *that* IF function removed.:

$$=IF(A22>\$A\$3,"THEN X",\$B\$2)$$

And so on and so on until I've found the part that was written incorrectly Does that make sense?

Remember when working with nested IF functions: slow and steady wins the race. Take it one step at a time. Test your possible outcomes. Don't get frustrated. Draw a diagram if you have to.

Okay, now on to COUNTIFS.

The COUNTIFS Function

Notation: COUNTIFS(criteria_range1, criteria1, [criteria_range2, criteria2],…)

Excel Definition: Counts the number of cells specified by a given set of conditions or criteria.

COUNTIFS will count the number of times your conditions are met in a selected range of cells. It does not have a calculation range like SUMIFS, AVERAGEIFS, etc. that we're going to discuss after this, because there's nothing to perform a calculation on. It's just counting how many times your conditions are met in the specified range of cells.

If you set more than one condition, the criteria ranges for all of the conditions must be the same size. To set just one condition only provide one criteria range and criteria.

You may run into COUNTIF in older versions of Excel or when only one condition is being used, but with COUNTIF and COUNTIFS the order of the inputs are identical so that shouldn't trip you up.

If you reference multiple conditions, your criteria do not have to be of the same type. Criteria can use numeric values (24 or "24"), cell references (A1), expressions (">42"), or text ("how").

Cell references and numbers do not need to be in quotation marks, but expressions and text references do.

For example:

$$=COUNTIFS(A1:A5,B2)$$

says to count how many times the values in Cells A1 through A5 are the same as the value in Cell B2.

$$=COUNTIFS(A1:A5,"YES")$$

says to count how many times the values in Cells A1 through A5 are the text YES. It will only count those instances where the full value in the cell matches the value given in the quotes. So a cell that says YES, PLEASE would not be counted. Nor would one that has YES followed by an extra space. It has to be an exact match unless you use wildcards, which we'll cover in a moment.

$$=COUNTIFS(A1:A5,">20")$$

says to count how many cells between Cell A1 and Cell A5 have a numeric value greater than 20. Note that even though the criteria is related to a number value that it's still shown in quotes because it's an expression. (If you had =COUNTIFS(A1:A5,20), which looks for any cells with a value equal to 20, you wouldn't need the quotes but you could still use them.)

If you want to reference a cell for your criteria but you also want to use a greater than or less than symbol, you need to combine the two using an ampersand (&).

For example

$$=COUNTIFS(A1:A5,">="&G2)$$

would count how many times the cells in the range from Cell A1 to Cell A5 contain a value that is greater than or equal to the value in Cell G2.

You can also use wildcards with the COUNTIFS function if your condition relates to a text value.

The asterisk (*) represents any number of characters or spaces. If you simply wanted to count any cell that contains text you would write that as

$$=COUNTIFS(A1:A5,"*")$$

It can also be used in combination with other letters to, for example, count any entry where there is an e. You would write that as

$$=COUNTIFS(A1:A5,"*e*")$$

The asterisks on either side of the e say to look for any cells where there is an e anywhere. If it were just on one side or the other then Excel would only look for words that starts with an e (e*) or ended with an e (*e).

If you want to count entries of a certain text length you can use the question mark (?) as a wildcard. It represents one single character. So

=COUNTIFS(A1:A5,"???")

would count all cells in the range from Cell A1 through A5 where the entry is three letters or spaces long. (It doesn't work with numbers.)

If you actually need to find an asterisk or question mark you can do so by using the tilde (~) before the mark you need. So ~? or ~* will look for an actual question mark or an actual asterisk

Always test different scenarios to make sure the count is counting everything you want it to but also not more than you want it to. (And be sure you've covered all possible scenarios in your testing, a mistake I know I've made at least once.)

Those were instances that would all work with COUNTIF or COUNTIFS because there was only one condition that needed to be met. Let's walk through a couple of scenarios that use multiple criteria now.

To count based upon multiple criteria, you simply include additional ranges and additional criteria for each one.

When you do so, the criteria range for all of your conditions must be the same size. So if your first cell range is A1:B25, then your other cell ranges must also be two columns wide and 25 rows long.

Ranges do not have to be adjacent, but they do have to be the same size.

The way the count is performed is it looks at all first cells in each of the criteria ranges and sees if the criteria for the first cell in each range is met.

If so, that entry is counted. If not, it isn't. It then moves on to the second cell in each of the criteria ranges and checks to see if all of the second cells meet the specified criteria. And so on and so on.

Each time all of the criteria are met, Excel counts that as 1.

Let's walk through an example to see this in action. I've created a table that has columns for State and Total Purchases for six customers and I want to count how many of my customers are both in Alabama (AL) and spent $250 or more. State is in Column A, Total Purchases is in Column B. The data is in Rows 2 through 7 with the header row in Row 1.

The function we need is:

=COUNTIFS(A1:A7,"AL",B1:B7,">=250")

Here it all is:

	A	B	C	D
1	State	Total Purchases		Customers From AL Who Spent At Least $250
2	AL	$ 275.00		3
3	AL	$ 250.00		Cell D2: =COUNTIFS(A1:A7,"AL",B1:B7,">=250")
4	AZ	$ 110.00		
5	AL	$ 95.00		
6	AR	$ 250.00		
7	AL	$ 300.00		

Our answer is 3 even though there were four potential purchases from AL and four purchases for $250 or more. Only three purchases met both conditions.

Let's break that down.

The first criteria range is A1 through A7. (We could have just as easily used A2 through A7 but it doesn't matter in this case if I include the header row since it won't meet my count criteria.) Those are the entries with our State values in them.

We told Excel we wanted to count any entry where the state is "AL".

The second criteria range is B1 through B7. That's our Total Purchases.

And we told Excel that for that range we wanted to count any time when a value was greater than or equal to $250. That's written as ">=250".

(Since this is a number and not a cell range we don't need the ampersand to combine the two.)

Excel then started with Cells A2 and B2 and determined whether both conditions were met. In this case, yes, so that first observation was counted. It continued onward like that to the end. Cells A5 and B5 only met one condition so were not counted. Same with Cells A6 and B6.

But Cells A3 and B3 as well as A7 and B7 did meet both conditions so were counted to give a total count of 3.

Remember, it's always a good idea to test your results against your data. So if I had a thousand rows of data I was using this formula on, I might write it to just cover ten rows first so I could test that it was working as expected before expanding to a sample size too big for me to judge easily. (Although with most of these you could use the filter options to filter your data to the same criteria you're using in your formula and then count, average, sum, etc. the results to double-check. That's another option.)

Okay. On to SUMIFS.

The SUMIFS Function

Notation: SUMIFS(sum_range, criteria_range1, criteria1, [criteria_range2, criteria2],…)

Excel Definition: Adds the cells specified by a given set of conditions or criteria.

SUMIFS allows you to sum the values in a range when multiple conditions are met. It can also work with just one condition if you only provide one criteria and one criteria range.

The first input is the range of cells that contain the values you want to add together. The second input is the range of cells that contain the values for your first criteria. The third input is the criteria itself. And then you just keep adding range of cells and condition that needs to be met until you have all of your criteria.

(Be careful if you ever do need to work with SUMIF which was this function's precursor, because the inputs are provided in a different order in SUMIF versus SUMIFS and SUMIF had less restraints than SUMIFS does.)

You can enter up to 127 conditions that need to be met before your values will be summed.

When using SUMIFS your sum range and the criteria ranges you use need to be the same size. They do not need to be next to one other or in any specific order on the worksheet, but they do need to cover the same number of rows and columns each.

SUMIFS can use a number (22 or "22"), an expression ("<13"), a text-based condition ("YES"), or a cell reference (H1) for the sum criteria. For anything except a single number or a cell reference, be sure to use quotation marks around your criteria.

You also don't have to use the same type of condition for each range. So you can use an expression for your first condition, a cell reference for your second, and a text-based condition for your third.

For text-based criteria, you can also use wildcards. The asterisk (*) represents any number of characters, the question mark (?) represents a single character, and the tilde (~) is used to distinguish when you're actually searching for an asterisk or question mark.

(See the COUNTIFS discussion for more detailed examples of all of the above.)

Here is a simple SUMIFS function with two conditions:

=SUMIFS(A1:A25,B1:B25,"USD",C1:C25,">10")

This would sum the values in Cells A1 through A25 if the value in the corresponding cells in Cells B1 through B25 contain "USD" and the values in Cells C1 through C25 are greater than 10. For Cell A1 it would look to Cells B1 and C1, for Cell A2 it would look to Cells B2 and C2, and so on and so on.

SUMIFS is one of the functions that I use the most.

For example, I use it in my budget worksheet to sum the amount I still owe on my bills each month.

I'll list all of my bills due for the month in Column A, whether I pay them with cash or with a credit card in Column B, the amount due in Column C, and I'll put an X when the bill is paid in Column D.

The SUMIFS formula I use is then:

=SUMIFS(C1:C10,B1:B10,"CASH",D1:D10,"")

That says sum the values in Column C if the values in Column B are "CASH" and Column D is blank. That lets me know how much cash I need in my bank account before those bills hit. As far as Excel is concerned Cash and CASH are the same. It is not case-sensitive.

The other place I use this is with my payables from publishing. I am usually owed money at any given time in about five different currencies and from about ten different sources. I have a worksheet where I sum the amount owed in each currency that I haven't yet been paid using a formula similar to the one above. In this case the formula for my USD payments is:

=SUMIFS(B$3:B$91,D$3:D$91,"USD",E$3:E$91,"")

This says to sum the values in Cells B3 through B91 if the values in Cells D3 through D91 are USD and the values in those cells in Column E are blank. I use Column E to check off when I receive a payment, so once payment is received that cell is no longer blank for that particular row.

I have a formula like this for each of the currencies I'm owed money in (CAD, AUD, INR, EUR, GBP, etc.) which is what the $ signs help with. This way I can just copy the formula to however many rows I need and all I have to update is the currency abbreviation.

Or even better yet, I can use a cell reference for that USD, say K2, and then when I copy the formula down it just references that same column but the new row so the currency abbreviation updates without any more effort from me.

=SUMIFS(B$3:B$91,D$3:D$91,K2,E$3:E$91,"")

That's just two examples of the power of SUMIFS. If you start to think about it, there are any number of places you can use it.

The AVERAGEIFS Function

Notation: AVERAGEIFS(average_range, criteria_range1, criteria1, [criteria_range2, criteria2],…)

Excel Definition: Finds average (arithmetic mean) for the cells specified by a given set of conditions or criteria.

The AVERAGEIFS function works just like SUMIFS except it takes an *average* of the values when a specified criteria is met. And just like SUMIFS and SUMIF, the order of the inputs in AVERAGEIFS differs from the order of the inputs in AVERAGEIF, so keep that in mind if you ever run into AVERAGEIF.

The inputs for the function are the range of cells that contain the values you want to average followed by the range of cells for your first condition and then the first condition parameters. If you want to use multiple criteria you then list the next range of cells and the next condition and so on and so on up to a total of 127 times.

Your average range and criteria range(s) must all be the same size and shape.

Your criteria do not have to be of the same type and can reference numeric values (24 or "24"), cells (A1), expressions (">42"), or text ("how").

Cell references and numbers do not need to be in quotation marks, expressions and text references do.

As with SUMIFS and COUNTIFS, you can use wildcards for text-based criteria. See the COUNTIFS description for examples.

For a value to be included in the average calculation, all of the conditions you specify must be met.

Be careful with empty cells, blanks, or text values where numbers are expected as these may generate an error message rather than a calculation or may impact the calculation.

(See the Excel help screen for the function for a full listing of the errors and adjustments that Excel makes. Always check a formula against a small sample of data to make sure you're getting the result you want.)

AVERAGEIFS evaluates TRUE values as 1 and FALSE values as 0.

The function will not work if the values in the average_range cannot be translated into numbers.

An example of using AVERAGEIFS might be if you were looking at student grades and wanted to see average score across teacher name and student gender to identify potential gender bias and/or overall score bias across teachers.

To do this, I'm going to build a table that has Test Score in Column A, Teacher Name in Column B, and Gender in Column C. Next, I'll build a table that has F and M in the header row on either side of a listing of the teacher names.

Finally I can then use AVERAGEIFS to pull into the second table the average score for female (F) and male (M) students for each teacher.

Here it is:

	A	B	C	D	E	F	G	H	I	J	K
1	**Score**	**Teacher**	**Gender**								
2	50	Smith	F								
3	49	Barker	M			**F**		**M**			
4	68	Vasquez	F			80.25	**Smith**	84.50			
5	75	Smith	M			90.00	**Barker**	68.67			
6	90	Barker	F			68.00	**Vasquez**	76.00			
7	94	Smith	M								
8	93	Barker	M		Cell F4:	=AVERAGEIFS($A$1:$A$13,$B$1:$B$13,G4,$C$1:$C$13,$F$3)					
9	91	Smith	F		Cell H4:	=AVERAGEIFS($A$1:$A$13,$B$1:$B$13,G4,$C$1:$C$13,$H$3)					
10	76	Vasquez	M								
11	82	Smith	F								
12	64	Barker	M								
13	98	Smith	F								

By putting the F and M values in Cells F3 and H3 to match the values in the Gender column in Column C I was able to reference those values with my formula. Same with the teacher last names in Column G.

The formula used in Cell F4 (for female students of Teacher Smith) is:

=AVERAGEIFS($A$1:$A$13,$B$1:$B$13,$G4,$C$1:$C$13,$F$3)

What that's saying is, average the values in Cells A1 through A13 where the values in Cells B1 through B13 are equal to the teacher name in Cell G4 and the gender of the student listed in Cells C1 through C13 is equal to the value in Cell F3.

By using the $ signs in the formula I can then copy the formula down to the other two rows in that table without making any other changes.

I did have to adjust the reference to $F$3 when I then copied the formula over to Column H for the male side and make that $H$3.

But by using $G4 I didn't have to adjust the reference to the teacher name when I copied it over.

Done. (Not statistically robust because we don't have enough data to really draw any sort of conclusion at all, but you can see how it could be interesting with enough data and really doesn't take all that much time to create.)

Don't forget, too, that AVERAGEIFS can be used with a single condition as well. So you could use it to calculate the average customer order amount for each state if you had a list of states, for example.

$$=AVERAGEIFS(A1:A1000,B1:B1000,"CO")$$

Would take the average of the values in Cells A1 through A1000 where the value in Column B was "CO".

(If you're ever trying to do a quick double-check of your values with AVERAGEIFS you can select the cells that it should be averaging and look on the bottom right side of your Excel screen and you should see values for Average, Count, and Sum for the selected cells. If Excel doesn't see your entries as numbers it will only show a count value.)

That's AVERAGEIFS, now on to MINIFS.

The MINIFS Function

Notation: MINIFS(min_range, criteria_range1, criteria1, [criteria_range2, criteria2],…)

Excel Definition: Returns the minimum value among cells specified by a given set of conditions or criteria.

The MINIFS function is a new function in Excel 2019. It works just like COUNTIFS, SUMIFS, and AVERAGEIFS except its purpose is to return the minimum value in a range of cells.

The inputs into the function are similar to the other functions we already discussed. The first input is the range with the values where your minimum value will be found. The next input is the range for your first condition. The third input is the condition. And so on and so forth up to 127 conditions.

As with the other functions, your min_range and criteria ranges need to all be the same size.

Your criteria do not have to be of the same type and can reference numeric values (24 or "24"), cells (A1), expressions (">42"), or text ("how"). Cell references and numbers do not need to be in quotation marks, expressions and text references do. And you can use wildcards for text-based criteria.

See the COUNTIFS description for examples of the various criteria types and wildcards.

Also, be sure your ranges are properly aligned. In the help section for this one they show an example where the ranges are not aligned and the function still works anyway because the ranges are the same size.

Also, the function will return a value of zero if there are not matches to the conditions you set, so be careful on that one because I can see a scenario where you might think zero was a legitimate result and it turns out that the zero result was just because the formula was written wrong.

So when would you use this? Well, let's go back to our grades by teacher and gender example and apply MINIFS instead of AVERAGEIFS.

	A	B	C	D	E	F	G	H	I	J	K
1	Score	Teacher	Gender								
2	50	Smith	F								
3	49	Barker	M				F		M		
4	68	Vasquez	F			50.00	Smith	75.00			
5	75	Smith	M			90.00	Barker	49.00			
6	90	Barker	F			68.00	Vasquez	76.00			
7	94	Smith	M								
8	93	Barker	M		Cell F4:	=MINIFS($A$2:$A$13,$B$2:$B$13,$G4,$C$2:$C$13,$F$3)					
9	91	Smith	F		Cell H4:	=MINIFS($A$2:$A$13,$B$2:$B$13,$G4,$C$2:$C$13,$H$3)					
10	76	Vasquez	M								
11	82	Smith	F								
12	64	Barker	M								
13	98	Smith	F								

The formula in Cell F4 becomes:

$$=MINIFS(\$A\$2{:}\$A\$13,\$B\$2{:}\$B\$13,\$G4,\$C\$2{:}\$C\$13,\$F\$3)$$

That's basically the same as the formula we used for AVERAGEIFS except we swapped out the function. What's interesting here is that we can see that for Barker, the minimum score for his female students is 90. That highlights a flaw in this data, which is that there is just one female student in Barker's class. And with Vasquez we can see that the averages and the minimums are the same as well and that's because there's only data for two students for Vasquez in the entire table, one male and one female.

Next we'll do the same for MAXIFS.

The MAXIFS Function

Notation: MAXIFS(max_range, criteria_range1, criteria1, [criteria_range2, criteria2],…)

Excel Definition: Returns the maximum value among cells specified by a given set of conditions or criteria.

MAXIFS was another new function added to Excel 2019. It works just like MINIFS except that it returns the maximum value in the range that meets the specified conditions.

Everything that held true for SUMIFS, AVERAGEIFS, and MINIFS also holds true for MAXIFS. The max_range and criteria_ranges need to be the same size and should be aligned correctly. If you have more than one condition they don't need to be the same type. You can use wildcards with text conditions. Criteria can reference numeric values, cells, expressions, or text.

Here is an example of applying MAXIFS to that same range of student scores that we applied it to for AVERAGEIFS and MINIFS:

	E	F	G	H	I	J	K
3		**F**		**M**			
4		98.00	**Smith**	94.00			
5		90.00	**Barker**	93.00			
6		68.00	**Vasquez**	76.00			
7							
8	**Cell F4:**	=MAXIFS($A$2:$A$13,$B$2:$B$13,$G4,$C$2:$C$13,$F$3)					
9	**Cell H4:**	=MAXIFS($A$2:$A$13,$B$2:$B$13,$G4,$C$2:$C$13,$H$3)					

The formula used in Cell F4 this time is:

$$=MAXIFS(\$A\$2:\$A\$13,\$B\$2:\$B\$13,\$G4,\$C\$2:\$C\$13,\$F\$3)$$

This time the values we see in the analysis table we built are the maximum scores for each gender for students in each teacher's class.

Again this serves to highlight the fact that for Barker there is only one female student and for Vasquez there is only one male and one female student.

This is noticeable when comparing the results across all three functions we've applied to the data.

In this table the Average column uses AVERAGEIFS, the Min column uses MINIFS, and the Max column uses MAXIFS. (And because of how I built the table I could just write each formula once and copy it down the rest of that column.)

Teacher	M/F	Average	Min	Max
Barker	F	90.00	90.00	90.00
Barker	M	68.67	49.00	93.00
Smith	F	80.25	50.00	98.00
Smith	M	84.50	75.00	94.00
Vasquez	F	68.00	68.00	68.00
Vasquez	M	76.00	76.00	76.00

Again, not a large enough data set to say anything about, but if it were a large data set, this is an excellent and easy way to compare grades across gender and teacher. It could as easily be used for sales performance by salesperson by month, product performance, etc.

Once you master one of these advanced IF functions you see that they all work pretty much the same way and so you can pick whichever one best suits your needs and be comfortable using it.

Conclusion

Alright. That was IF Functions. If you want to learn more niche topics, check out the rest of the series which covers PivotTables, Charts, and Conditional Formatting. Or if you want to now explore a broader range of topics you can choose *Excel 2019 Intermediate* or *Excel 2019 Formulas & Functions* which cover those topics and more.

Appendix A: Basic Terminology

Most of the terminology I use is pretty standard but I think I do have a few quirks in how I refer to things, so be sure to do a quick skim of this section just to make sure we're on the same page. This is meant to be a refresher only. These terms were initially taught in *Excel 2019 Beginner*.

Column

Excel uses columns and rows to display information. Columns run across the top of the worksheet and, unless you've done something funky with your settings, are identified using letters of the alphabet.

Row

Rows run down the side of the worksheet and are numbered starting at 1 and up to a very high number. In Excel 2019 that number is 1048576.

Cell

A cell is a combination of a column and row that is identified by the letter of the column it's in and the number of the row it's in. For example, Cell A1 is the cell in the first column and first row of a worksheet.

Click

If I tell you to click on something, that means to use your mouse (or trackpad) to move the cursor on the screen over to a specific location and left-click or right-click on the option. (See the next definition for the difference between left-click and right-click).

If you left-click, this generally selects the item. If you right-click, this generally creates a dropdown list of options to choose from. If I don't tell you which to do, left- or right-click, then left-click.

Left-click/Right-click

If you look at your mouse or your trackpad, you generally have two flat buttons to press. One is on the left side, one is on the right. If I say left-click that means to press down on the button on the left. If I say right-click that means press down on the button on the right. (If you're used to using Word or Excel you may already do this without even thinking about it. If that's the case then think of left-click as what you usually use to select text and right-click as what you use to see a menu of choices.)

Spreadsheet

I'll try to avoid using this term, but if I do use it, I'll mean your entire Excel file. It's a little confusing because it can sometimes also be used to mean a specific worksheet, which is why I'll try to avoid it as much as possible.

Worksheet

This is the term I'll use as much as possible. A worksheet is a combination of rows and columns that you can enter data in. When you open an Excel file, it opens to Sheet1.

Workbook

I don't use this term often, but it may come up. A workbook is an Excel file and can contain multiple worksheets. The default file type for an Excel 2019 workbook is a .xlsx file type.

Formula Bar

This is the long white bar at the top of the screen with the $f\chi$ symbol next to it.

Tab

I refer to the menu choices at the top of the screen (File, Home, Insert, Page Layout, Formulas, Data, Review, View, and Help) as tabs. Note how they look like folder tabs from an old-time filing system when selected? That's why.

Data

I use data and information interchangeably. Whatever information you put into a worksheet is your data or data set.

Select

If I tell you to "select" cells, that means to highlight them. Same with text.

Arrow

If I say that you can "arrow" to something that just means to use the arrow keys to navigate from one cell to another.

Cell Notation

We may end up talking about cell ranges in this book. Excel uses a very specific type of cell notation. We already mentioned that a cell is referenced based upon the letter of its column and the number of its row. So A1 is the cell in Column A and Row 1. (When used as cell notation you don't need to include Cell before the A1.)

To reference a range of cells Excel uses the colon (:) and the comma (,). A colon between cells means "through". So A1:B25 means all of the cells between Cell A1 and Cell B25 which is all of the cells in Columns A and B and Rows 1 through 25. A comma means and. So A1,B25 would be Cells A1 and B25 only.

When in doubt, go into Excel, type = and the cell range, hit enter, and then double-click back into that cell. Excel will highlight all of the cells in the range you entered.

Dialogue Box

I will sometimes refer to dialogue boxes. These are the boxes that occasionally pop up with additional options for you to choose from for a particular task.

Paste Special – Values

Paste Special - Values is a special type of pasting option which I often use to remove formulas from my data or to remove a pivot table but keep the table it created. If I tell you to Paste Special - Values that means use the Values paste option which is the one with a 123 on the clipboard.

Dropdown

I will occasionally refer to a dropdown or dropdown menu. This is generally a list of potential choices that you can select from if you right-click on your worksheet or on one of the arrows next to an option in the tabs at the top. For example, if you go to the Home tab and click on the arrow under Paste, you will see additional options listed in a paste dropdown menu.

Task Pane

I am going to call the separate standalone pane that appears on the right-hand side of the screen on occasion a task pane. These appear for PivotTables, charts, and the Help function.

About the Author

M.L. Humphrey is a former stockbroker with a degree in Economics from Stanford and an MBA from Wharton who has spent close to twenty years as a regulator and consultant in the financial services industry.

You can reach M.L. Humphrey at:

mlhumphreywriter@gmail.com

or at

www.mlhumphrey.com

www.ingramcontent.com/pod-product-compliance
Lightning Source LLC
Chambersburg PA
CBHW060510060326
40689CB00020B/4694